To Loveavo! [handwritten inscription]

Won't Be Long

Poems Short,
Poems Shorter,
Poems Shortest

J.R. Solonche [signature]

DEERBROOK EDITIONS

PUBLISHED BY
Deerbrook Editions
P.O. Box 542
Cumberland, ME 04021
www.deerbrookeditions.com
www.issuu.com/deerbrookeditions

FIRST EDITION
ISBN: 978-0-9975051-3-9
© 2016 by J.R. Solonche
All right reserved.

Book & cover design by Jeffrey Haste.

Acknowledgements

Some of the poems in this book first appeared in the following periodicals:

Adirondack Review: Blue Butterfly
Chronogram: Agnosticism; Birthday (under a different title); Poem at 7:30 AM
Four and Twenty: At the Gym; Positional; Simile
Ginosko: The Turn
Ha!: Envy (under a different title)
Loch Raven Review: Physical
Matchbook Poetry: Neighbor
Obsession: Question for the Oracle
Poet Lore: Poem Beginning with a Line by Philip Larkin
Poetry Jumps Off the Shelf /
            Woodrow Hall Editions: Private Property
Poetry Superhighway: Art; English
Tattoo Highway: Very Short Speech for Lazarus
Vain Magazine: Comet; So Far

Part One

Poems Short

Patriotism

I don't own an American flag.
I never have.
I grew up in an apartment
building in the Bronx.
Nobody owned a flag.
Now that I live on a road in the country,
all my neighbors fly the flag.
Except one.
Like them, he does have a flagpole
with a flag hanging on it
in front of his house.
But he says he isn't flying it.
He says he's lynching it.

Physical

The stethoscope, his cold third ear,
pressed against my chest, "Take
a breath," my physician says as
though offering me a box full of
his own collection of breaths, each
one better than any of mine. "Breathe
in, hold it," he says, so this one
I roll around in my mouth, such
a fine brandy of breath he
has poured just for me.

To My Desk

I have faith in you.
I trust you not to reveal them, our secrets.
You are hard and stubborn and loyal.
I know you will never tell
the things you have overheard.
No, not even if they torture you,
burn you with cigarettes,
cut you with razors,
or break, one at a time,
so painfully slowly,
your smooth, slender legs.

Touch

. . . the last sense to fade at life's culmination.

So is this how it will be, Death,
when we finally get married?
I will not see your face when I lift your veil?
I will not hear you whisper my name?
I will not smell your breath on my face?
I will not taste the wine?
I will only feel your hand in mine,
your touch, for only as long as it takes to say,
"I do"?

His Nose Answers Dr. Williams

No, I cannot be decent.
No, I cannot reserve my ardors
for something less unlovely than that rank
odor of a passing spring.
Yes, I must taste everything!
Yes, I must know everything!
Yes, I must have a part in everything!
And don't worry, Doc.
Flossie will care for us
if we continue in these ways.

Blue Butterfly

I was outside reading.
A blue butterfly settled on the table.
The opening and closing of its blue wings
looked like a small blue book opening and
closing.
Then it looked like a blue eye opening and
closing.
Then it looked like the blue book.
Then it looked like the blue eye.
Then the blue book.
The blue eye.

March

It is warm.
The snow is melting fast.
All three feet of it.
The water rushes down
the gutter and out
into the snow
still on the grass.
The water
is a liquid knife
working fast
through the snow.
The sun is warmed up
and working fast.
Ah, surgeon of
the hot hands, how
you save the life of life.

I Want to Die Like a Navajo

I want to die like a Navajo.
I want to sign the poem,
"When that time comes
when my last breath leaves
me, I choose to die
in peace to meet Shi' dy' in."
Then, as I will no longer
be on Mother earth,
you may wash up,
take your corn pollen,
and go on with life.

Comet

Do not imagine that
you can imagine it,
the man standing,
two thousand years
from now when it
will appear again
where you are standing
looking northwest
at this bearded star.
This man is beyond you,
what he is imagining
beyond you. Nothing
will be the same.
Not standing.
Not imagining.
Not men.

The Perfect Place

The perfect place
is not a piece of paper.
It is not a book.
The perfect place
is an old wall,
but whitewashed new,
which the citizens
come upon suddenly,
taken unawares,
as they turn the corner
of their crowded city,
out of the corner
of their eye.

False Spring

Don't you hate spring
when it is not?
When it sticks its nose
into winter's business?
Don't you hate sunshine
when it is disingenuous?
Don't you hate melt
when it doesn't go all the way?
Don't you hate lies
no matter who the liar is?

You Never Know Which Rain

You never know which rain
will be the last of fall's rain.
But I'm sure it isn't today's rain.
It is too warm.
The maples aren't yet done.
The year needs to bleed some
more before doctor winter
arrives with his pure
white bandages,
with his sterile needles
filled with sleep.

To Sleep

Death's dwarf,
headstone headliner's warm up act,
What sort of fool do you take me for, pal?
While I each night entrust myself to you,
my head knee-deep in your lap,
I wait for eternity to wield,
behind your back, its ax,
light as the feather in your cap.

As to What He Has Done

As to what he has done and what he has not:
He has taught some things to some
but has left much more
untaught to many more.
He has written some words
but has left many more unwritten.
Many nights has he not slept thinking,
"What does better mean?"

On the Wall of
the Tibetan Arts Store

On the wall of the Tibetan arts store,
I saw a mask of myself.
"How much?" I asked.
"It costs your soul," said the owner.
I bought it, put it on and left.
I wear it all the time except at night.
While asleep.
Or not asleep.

Georgia O'Keeffe, *City Night*

It is not just in the lilies
and the irises and the shells.
It is also here, in the dark cleft,
the mysterious canyon of skyscrapers.
Eroticism ironed out, squared off, hurried.
Even here in the cool glowing clitoris of
moon.

Stand Perfectly Still

Stand perfectly still
beneath the wild cherry tree
toward the end of April,
when it opens its hands
to let fall the white
blossoms petal by petal,
singly and in clusters,
and you will know
what it means to be dizzy
while standing perfectly still.

Who Whispered

Who whispered
into the ear of
the wild cherry tree
that it blushed
rosy pink for
a whole week?
Who told it
that ribald tale
of the old man
and his young wife
that it burst out in
such a white belly
laugh of blossoms?

The Flowers at Night

The flowers at night are all the same.
And at night, the trees are all the same.
So too are the clouds at night the same.
Only the wind at night is different,
so different as it moans its secrets
to the unwilling who cannot turn away.

The Names

One spelled Dickinson with an *e*.
Another spelled Eliot with two *l*'s.
A third spelled Whitman without an *h*.
If nothing else, I said, spell the names right.
At least spell the names right.
If nothing else, I said.
The fucking names.

My Daughter Wants to Sit in the Shade

My daughter wants to sit in the shade.
My wife wants to sit in the sun.

We move the table half in shade, half in sun.
Problem solved.

Yin and yang, right?
Well, not exactly.

Yin, yang, and yin.
As I sit in both.

Poem on a Napkin

When the napkin is spread on my lap,
the poem is a map.

When the napkin is tucked in my shirt,
the poem is a flirt.

When the napkin wipes my lip,
the poem is a slip

of the tongue.

Across

Across the street
is a church
with a cross
above the door
and another
one on the roof
and glass crosses
in all the windows.
So many crosses,
I suppose
they want us
never to forget
who the boss is.

The Train

When the train begins, it is far away.
When the train ends, it is far away.
Only for a minute is
the train close enough to hear.
But it is only then that the train is what
far away sounds like.

Private Property

There are 57,308,738
square miles of land in the world.

That's 36,677,592,320 acres.

As decreed by Map 16, Block 2,
Lots 3 and 4, I own 0.50 acres.

This comes to 1/73,355,104,640th
of the land in the world.

Keep out!

Philosophy

The Pythagoreans worshiped number.
They believed that fire was made of 24
right angled triangles surrounded by 4
equilateral triangles composed of 6
right angled triangles.
But they thought about such things
only after the water boiled for morning coffee.

Aesthetics

The maker
of the door
is not concerned
with the room
into which
the door opens,
nor is he concerned
with the hall
upon which
the door closes.
These are
the concerns
of the maker
of the walls.

Skunk

Good morning, dawn
of white striped sun-
rise, let you be now my moral model
for the world,
for the worst of us, skunk, animal
best black and white,
of a better world whose only evil
is an evil smell.

The Hummingbird

drinks from one impatiens,
then from another, and then from a third.

Finally, it goes to the feeder
filled with sugar water,
hangs around, but does not drink.

Why should we be insulted?
We also planted the impatiens there.

Jim and I

were drinking
and talking about death,
which is the best way.
"When the time comes,
I hope I have the courage
to spit in his eye," I said.
"When the time comes,
I hope I have the spit,"
said Jim.

Spring

When the days get longer,
the birds know it is time to sing.
There is something in the mind
of the bird that responds
to light's lengthening.
As to what that is,
biologists are still in the dark.

The Dogwood Trees

White is
the only color
they require
here.
They need
not aspire
to any other
in such a sea
of greens.
Even then,
less than
their best
is quite
all right,
this right-
on-target off-
white.

Poem Beginning with a Line by Philip Larkin

Heaviest of flowers, the head
holds everything. Even what we believed
was long ago forgotten is still there,
beyond reason,
a scent, slight, stale, but recognizable
under the thinning sweetness of decay,
season after season after season.

Walk

"Look, there's a deer skull," I said,
pointing to the deer skull by the side of the
road.

"Look, there's a beer skull," Jim said,
pointing to the Coors can by the side of the
road.

Where

I tree stands where I want to stand.
The wind walks where I want to walk.

Very well.
I will stand in another place.

Very well.
I will wait for the wind to pass.

I Almost Spilled

my coffee on
the desk just now.
To which of
you should
I be grateful then
for sparing me
embarrassment?
You god
of coffee?
Or you
goddess of
embarrassment?

I Asked the Guy on Purgatory Road

I asked the guy on Purgatory Road
why on earth he built a house so close
to the railroad tracks up there.
I grew up on Jerome Avenue in the Bronx,
he said, which explained everything.

On the Wall

in one of the stalls
in the men's room,
someone wrote,
"I want my sweater
back." Or perhaps
it was, "I want my
sweetheart back."
It was hard to read.

A Cloud

of starlings
arrives out
of the blue
out of the blue,
settles down
in the trees
out back
but briefly,
then leaves,
backs out
once again
the blue out
of the black.

Office

I went to the office.
Jim was there with a student.
He was quoting Hume.
"Sorry, you're busy.
I'll come back," I said.
"No, it's okay, sit down," Jim
said. "I'm humoring him."

Mountain Pose

My feet are planted firmly on the earth.
But I have no feet.

My head is risen higher than the clouds.
But I have no head.

At last, I am a mountain.

To a Colleague Recently Retired

Tell me the truth.
So now that you have all this time
on your hands,
don't you wish,
even a little bit, that you still had
all those hands on your time?

Knowledge

Knowing how paper is made,
or how ink is made,
or how a pen is made,
has nothing to do with how
a poem is made.
How lucky for the poet.

English

How can you say anything bad
about a language that lets you sing
"I've been beaten down for so long
Lawd, Lawd, I feel all beaten up"?

Q and A

Did He who made the lamb make thee?
Yes, He who made the lamb made me.
But made me first, his masterstroke.
And then the lamb, his little joke.

At the Next Table

At the next table,
a man is writing on his laptop.

He looks just like Gary Snyder.
Do not be fooled.

This means nothing at all.
For example,

I'm told I look
just like Charles Wright.

Manhattan

I don't care what
the historians say.

I don't care what
the sociologists say.

I don't care what
the anthropologists say.

Jericho, first city,
is the gravestone of the earth.

1939 Photo of Mount Rushmore

Teddy Roosevelt isn't quite done.
Scaffolding still covers his face.
He looks like Yogi Berra.
Or the umpire calling the third strike
on a disbelieving Jefferson.

Belief

I never believed
a black
could be blacker
than the black
of crows
until I saw
a crow fly
through rain
blacker
than the black
of crows.

About Those True Believers

Do not be fooled because they're nice.
They are the ones who drug reason on the
altar of faith,
the ones who truly practice human sacrifice.

The Differences

The differences
between the earth
and the world are
many, but the only
one you need to know
is the earth rotates
and the world spins.

Words

"If I only had
a larger vocabulary,"
I have thought
more than once,
as though I could
do what I want
through sheer
weight of numbers.

Hot Work

The pileated
woodpecker
with his head
of fire chisels
away so hot
that a mound
of tree ash
has formed
around the base
of the ash tree.

The Daffodils

The daffodils
have bloomed
golden blood
so fast in the bed
by Morrison
it looks like
the morning sun
has cut its finger
climbing the fence.

Upper West Side

Why do I think the guy
washing the silver PT Cruiser
in front of his brownstone on 90th
wants me to feel like a loser?

If the Jet

streaking across
the sky
from east to west
sounds
as natural to us
as the cricket
in the grass,
who is to blame?

Emily Dickinson in Hell

I'm in Hell – Forever – now –
And you – are you here too?
Then there's a Billion of us!
Do tell! Hell's so – Popular – with Populace!

Wild Turkeys

Like dirty oil
from an old
truck, the wild
turkeys leak
out of the woods
and across the road,
black drop
by black drop.

Every April

the cherry tree
puts on the same
white wedding
gown to marry
the sun, and
every year
I write the same
epithalamion.

Bees in the Wild Cherry Tree

In my next life,
I want to come back
as the honey bees.
Yes, you heard me right.
Not one bee.
All of them.

So Many Goldfinches

were scattered
around the feeders
this morning,
I thought the sun
was in a head-on
collision with
last night
and shattered.

The Artist's Mother

The real name
of James McNeill Whistler's
painting is
Arrangement in Gray and Black No. 1.

I've never seen No. 2.
Have you?

Means to Ends

Would you make
a better bed
of roses
if the only way
to do it
was to make
a sharper
crown of thorns?

Part Two

Poems Shorter

Poem Based on Five Words Given
to My Daughter by Her First
Grade Teacher: *Like, our, play, saw, was*

Like me, you are tormented by words.
Our sky is two skies.
Blackbirds play letters in them.
In yours, *saw.*
In mine, *was.*

Adirondacks

The day after
returning home
from the Adirondacks,
I could not remember
if they had been
miles of mountains
or mountains
of miles.

Clarity

When at last everything becomes clear,
you will see,
for the very first time,
that it had never really been everything.

Mowing

I hate this.
I can't tell you
how much I hate this.
But the sun feels good on my face.
And I'm alive.

Enough

Today there wasn't
enough sunlight
to fill
my coffee cup,
yet the potted paper whites
followed it
from window
to window to window.

Adage

Okay, okay.
One cannot make
a silk purse
from a sow's ear,
but one can
make a sow's ear
purse from
a sow's ear.

Greenhouse

If it's so perfect
in there,
why does
the crimson
cyclamen
pressing
the glass
look like
it wants
to get out?

So Far

So far humans
have not
come so far.
Not really.
Not according
to the science
of such things,
the science
so far.

Vieux Quebec

"I can see the old city,"
my wife says.

"It doesn't look old to me,"
I say.

"Maybe they painted it,"
says my daughter.

Review

He has no confidence
in verbs and nouns,
so he sends them out
surrounded by
adverbs and adjectives,
their bodyguards.

Exactly

It is neither
too late

nor too early
but exactly

the right time
to be either

too late
or too early.

Envy

I envy those poets
who invite

their poems
and their poems arrive.

Hell, I have
to subpoena mine.

The Grand Canyon

What a joke
the gods
must have told
to cause
the earth to laugh
so hard
it split its
side laughing.

On the Corner

"Even in my dream,
I hated my hair," one said.

"So what the hell's
the use of dreams?" said the other.

Critics

Last night,
through the open
window,
I heard an owl
hissing.
Funny,
I didn't think
my dream
was all
that bad.

Watching

The more
I watch
the birds
from my window,
the more
I am convinced
that the wrong people
are people.

Emily Dickinson's Bedroom

Neat as a pin,
just like the poems
that prick the skin
and, drop by drop,
bleed us from within.

Some Things

are just
so crazy
to think about
that we
have no choice
except to
do them
without thinking.

Old Chinese Saying

Calling things by
their right names
is the first step on
the journey to wisdom.

Okay.
Now what?

Swamp

The half-submerged
log where yesterday
four turtles sunbathed
today has nothing
but a space
the size of four turtles.

Begonia

Little red headed stoic,
the begonia
keeps taking
the raindrops' beating
all morning,
even without
shoulders,
shrugging it off.

What the Ugly One Said

You are not
used to me.

I am for
another time.

And a different
generosity.

Art

John Coltrane
practiced so many
hours a day,
the reeds
of his saxophone
turned red.

At the Grave of Emily Dickinson

All the Dickinsons
have *DIED* on their stones.

She does not. Unique
as ever, she was *CALLED BACK*.

Short Speech for Cain

The kid
sacrificed a kid.
I wanted
to go one better,
so I sacrificed him
on my altar.

Old Hemlock

The old hemlock
is the campus
graybeard,
so how come
no one
thought to
put a bench
under it?

The Dream

In the dream
I was invisible
until I passed
through the world
of invisible mirrors
and saw myself.

Relativity

In the good dream,
I begged for my living.

In the bad dream,
I begged for my life.

The Difference

Prose is a 40-watt bulb.
Enough to read by.

Poetry is a 4000-watt floodlight.
Enough to blind you.

An Answer

When the rabbi in his sermon
said, "It is a sin
to desire completion,"
I left my religion.

On Being Told My Poems Seem Forced

You know, you're right.
They do indeed seem forced.
But there is a simple explanation.
My poems are my children.

Frost's *The Gum-Gatherer*

Robert sure had balls.
This gum-gatherer is none other
than Wordsworth's leech-gatherer
in flannel shirt and overalls.

Thistle Down

Before drifting
at the mercy
of the wind,
it is freed
by the justice
of the wind.

In the Office

We were talking about Mailer.
"He was so egotistical," I said.
"No, he was so ego-testicle," said Jim.

November First

May first's shorter twin.
Come on.

Let's go outside.
Let's see

what winter's
made of.

Dialogue

"No time like the present,"
said the surgeon

"No present like the time,"
agreed the patient.

Cinquain

Crocus.
Spring morning walk.
The lake ice nearly gone.
Suddenly a black shadow's wings:
Crow curse.

Sign of Spring

The stop sign
in the parking lot
is a single red rose
in a gray garden.

Aphorisms

Sometimes
sayings
have to
be said
out of
the need
to put
some
times
into words.

Part Three

Poems Shortest

December Morning

The snow
has turned
the world old
overnight.
Therefore
I will not
ask anything
of it today.

Neighbor

So many children
running around
in the yard,
we knew
he must
have been dying

When the Administrator

finally finished his inarticulate speech,
Jim blurted out,
"My sentiments approximately!"

Poem

Some things
need to be words,
and some
things need
to be
themselves,
including
words.

The Morning Freight

Did you see it?
No?

How well
it covers

its tracks.

Early January

The geese
are crying
in the distance.

Or is that the distance
crying in
the geese?

Confession

I am
faithful
to my
wife.
And that's
the long
and
the short
of it.

Question for the Oracle

Know thyself.
Okay.

Nothing in excess.
Okay.

But does that
include

knowing
thyself?

The Truth

So hypnotic,
I can't take
my eyes
off of it.

The pot is boiling.

Spring

My neighbor
removes
the cover from
his red Vette.

Ah!
First flower
of spring!

Of Wei Qingzhi

almost nothing
is known.

He planted 1000
chrysanthemums.

But that alone
is everything.

Defense

How do you expect
me to eat crow
with my foot
in my mouth?

Time

It is neither
yours
to give
nor mine
to receive,
yet
so warm
from our hands.

Birthday

I approach my
seventieth year,
slowly, carefully,
from behind,
so as not to
frighten it away.

Concert

The oratorio ended.
My daughter said,
"You have a bass clap, dad."

The Turn

I get to the corner.
I turn right and
cut the future
in half.

To Take

too much
for granted
first requires
too much
be left
for granted.

Hey

want to do
a good deed today?

Befriend a lonely
old poem.

A Lesson

First you are *brought* before a judge.
Then you are *taken* to prison.

From the Window

The rain off
the duck's back
was like water off
a duck's back.

Issa

It means *cup of tea,*
which, for most,
he is not.
Oh, unfortunately.

Disparity

Art is
part *party,*
part *star,*
part *dirty,*
part *ist,*
part *I pray.*

Poem at 5:01 a.m.

Most deaths
of natural causes
occur, scientists
say, between
3 and 5 am.

Richard Eberhart Dead at 101

Happily for us,
of poets it cannot be said
we outlive our usefulness.

October

It is April's opposite.
With new buds of death,
the trees flower yellow, orange, red.

News of the Passing of Grandmother Karp at 98

The doctor said heart failure.
We know better.

It was heart success.
Congratulations, Granny!

In Poetry

there are no
wrong words.

There are only
sour notes.

The Sky

without a cloud
is like the mind
without an idea.

Apology

What I had
in mind
is not
what I
had in
mind.

Epitaph for a Boxer

I couldn't
beat him
to death,
so I beat
him to death.

Simile

The good memory
sits heavily
on your mind
like a bad memory.

Shit Haiku

Again the toilet.
Many delicious dried plums.
But this haiku is shit.

Another Old Chinese Saying

What good are
one-thousand bows
if there is only
one arrow?

Agnosticism

I can be convinced,
but it will have to
be in person.

Departure

It left
before my
very eyes
right before
my very
eyes.

A Photo of Me

Shit, how I envy
all the millions
who died before
photography.

Poem at 7:30 a.m.

What can
be more
beautiful than
a red
frying pan?

News Item

Virgin Airlines Sells $250,000 Tickets For Five–Minute Space Flight

Now there's
a vacation
worth its
weightlessness
in gold.

March 14

Today is Einstein's birthday.
The sun is shining.

The Last Paradox

When it's time
to go,

there's no time
to go.

She Said He Said

She:
I remembered everything.

He:
I remembered you remembering everything.

Peace

Peace of body
is always
required for
peace of mind.

Last Request

I want to die
like there's
no tomorrow.

God Gives Hope
(Road Sign for the Calvary Assembly Church)

Hope we have already.
Who's giving the certainty?

Hell

is heaven's parody.
Unless it's the other way around.

Education

Some things
cannot be learned.

Learning,
for instance.

Positional

I'm under
no illusions.

I'm over them.

At the Gym

Working out
is not
working out.

Post-Coital

It all
comes
down to
this.

Time

One irreplaceable
moment
after another.

Excuses

I'm a poet.
What's yours?

Hamlet

Revenge play
with
a vengeance.

Pessimism

Time after time after time.

Optimism

Time before time before time.

Nowhere

The original word
for *here*.

To My Nose

Funny, you don't look Jewish.

No News

Good news all day today.

Good News

No news all day today.

The Philosophy of Apple

iI ithink itherefore iI iam.

Very Short Speech for a New Husband

Look, ma,
no hands.

The Secret

It goes
without
saying.

Politics

All poetry is local.

The Passing of a Noted Critic

Detraction
was
the attraction.

The Surest Way to Fool Yourself
into Believing Anything You
Want

Make up
your mind.

Very Short Speech for Lazarus

Jesus,
what
a dream.

Newspaper

Today's suicide note.

Nothing Sacred

All
holy.

In the Terminal

Interminable.